AMERICAN LEGENDS™

Clara Barton

Frances E. Ruffin

The Rosen Publishing Group's
PowerKids Press™
New York

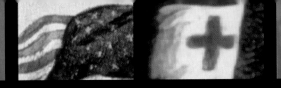

For my Aunt Juanita

Published in 2002 by The Rosen Publishing Group, Inc.
29 East 21st Street, New York, NY 10010

First Edition

Book Design: Michael de Guzman

Project Editor: Kathy Campbell

Photo Credits: pp. 4, 12, 20 © Bettmann/CORBIS; p. 7 © Jennie Woodcock; Reflections Photolibrary/CORBIS; pp. 8, 16 © CORBIS; p. 11 © National Park Service, Clara Barton National Historic Site; p. 15 © North Wind Pictures; p. 19 © CORBIS-BETTMANN.

Ruffin, Frances E.
Clara Barton / Frances E. Ruffin.— 1st ed.
    p. cm. — (American legends)
Includes index.
ISBN 0-8239-5825-6 (lib. bdg.)
1. Barton, Clara, 1821–1912—Juvenile literature. 2. Red Cross—United States—Biography—Juvenile literature.
3. Nurses—United States—Biography—Juvenile literature. 4. United States—History—Civil War, 1861–1865—Medical care—Juvenile literature. [1. Barton, Clara, 1821–1912. 2. Nurses. 3. Women—Biography.] I. Title. II. American legends (New York, N.Y.)
HV569.B3 R83 2002
361.7'634'092—dc21

                                                00-012447

Manufactured in the United States of America

Contents

Clara Barton's work as a nurse during the Civil War made her a famous figure in American history.

Clara Barton

During some of the fiercest battles of the **Civil War**, fought from 1861 to 1865, injured soldiers looked up to see a woman on the battlefield. The small, dark-haired woman in a blouse and long skirt was Clara Barton. Few women had ever seen the horrors of war that Clara Barton witnessed. She was often in danger. She had been injured and, on several occasions, had come close to being killed. This did not prevent Clara Barton from caring for the soldiers who needed her, whether their uniforms were **Union** blue or **Confederate** gray. Clara Barton was an American **legend**.

What Is a Legend?

A legend is a story that has come down to us from the past. A legend also can be a person we admire. **Legendary** people often have qualities that are so special, they are remembered even after they are no longer living. Clara Barton was a very brave woman. She was a **humanitarian**. During her life, she overcame many **obstacles** so that she could help others. She had been a teacher and then became a battlefield nurse. Clara Barton is most remembered, though, for starting the American Red Cross. Since 1881, this organization has helped people to **survive** and recover from wars and other disasters.

Reading about legends, or stories that come down to us from the past, is fun. Legends can include stories about real people or events from the past. They also can include parts of stories that might have been made up to make the legend more exciting.

This is a picture of Clara, at left, with her older sister Sally. Clara, the Bartons' youngest daughter, was a good student, but very shy as a child.

The Christmas Baby

Clarissa Harlowe Barton was born in North Oxford, Massachusetts, on December 25, 1821. She was the youngest of Sarah and Captain Stephen Barton's five children. Stephen Barton was a member of the Massachusetts State **Legislature**. The family was delighted with their Christmas baby, whom they called Clara. Her older sisters and brothers treated her like a china doll. Her mother, Sarah, was a hardworking woman who taught young Clara to cook, sew, and manage a home. Sarah felt that toys were **frivolous**. Clara's father, Captain Barton, liked to tell Clara about battle **strategies** from his experiences fighting in the Indian Wars during the 1770s.

A Little Nurse, A Teenage Teacher

When Clara was 10 years old, her 23-year-old brother, David, fell from the **rafters** of the family's barn. The serious accident left him ill with headaches and **fevers** for two years. During that time, Clara stayed home and took care of him. When he got better, she was proud that she had helped to nurse him back to health.

Clara was only 17 years old when she was appointed to teach in a one-room school. Clara taught 40 children in her class. Some of the older boys at the school were known for being bullies. On the first day, Clara won the respect of the class when she read a sermon from the Bible that said, in part, that one "must love one's enemies."

At an early age, Clara showed an interest in helping other people. She came from a family of schoolteachers and decided to follow the path to become a teacher.

Clara lived in the capital city of Washington, D.C., when Abraham Lincoln became president of the United States. Around 1860, the southern states began to talk about breaking away from the country over the issue of slavery.

A New Career

Clara Barton taught school for more than 15 years. During that time, she helped to open free schools for children from poor families. She also fought for higher salaries for female teachers. She was a much-loved, well-respected teacher. In 1854, Clara moved to Washington, D.C., and changed her **career**. She took a job in the Patent Office, copying secret papers. This government office examines claims to inventions. Clara was living in Washington in November 1860, when Abraham Lincoln was elected president of the United States. Before and after Lincoln's election, the issue of **slavery** had begun to divide the country. The country seemed headed for war.

A War Begins

In December 1860, South Carolina withdrew from the United States. South Carolina and, later, 10 other southern states formed the Confederate States of America. On April 12 and 13, 1861, Confederate forces fired on and took over Fort Sumter in South Carolina. President Lincoln called for 75,000 **volunteers** to put down that attack against the Union. By May 1861, the Civil War had begun. At the beginning of the war, Clara Barton helped the Union army by handing out food, clothing, bandages, and medicines. During a battle at Cedar Mountain, Virginia, in August 1862, Clara, alone, drove a wagon pulled by a mule to deliver the supplies to the battlefront.

On April 12, 1861, the Confederates began to fire on Fort Sumter in Charleston Harbor. This attack started the Civil War. Clara helped the Union effort during the war by delivering supplies to the wounded soldiers.

During the second battle of Bull Run, Clara and her friends took care of wounded and dying soldiers on both sides.

Bull Run

When the second battle of Bull Run at Manassas, Virginia, started on August 29, 1862, Clara invited four women to go to the front with her. The women traveled in a boxcar that had no seats or windows. They traveled all night, sitting in darkness. They rode surrounded by crates and barrels of supplies that were stacked to the ceiling. When the train came to a stop, they were greeted by a scene of horror. They saw a battlefield that reached to a far hillside. The field was covered with soldiers who were injured or dead. Clara and the women immediately began to work. They started to bandage the soldiers' wounds and give the men food and water.

Angel of the Battlefield

Near Fairfax, Virginia, thousands of soldiers lay in a bloody, rain-soaked field. Clara Barton and her four volunteers heard screams of pain. Most of the soldiers had not had food or water for two days. Clara prepared a mixture of hard army biscuits, crushed up and mixed with wine, water, and brown sugar, to give the soldiers. That winter, during a battle in Fredricksburg, Virginia, Clara came to the aid of both Union and Confederate soldiers. "I make **gruel**, not speeches; I write letters home for wounded soldiers, not political **addresses**," she said. An army surgeon who admired her efforts called Clara Barton the Angel of the Battlefield.

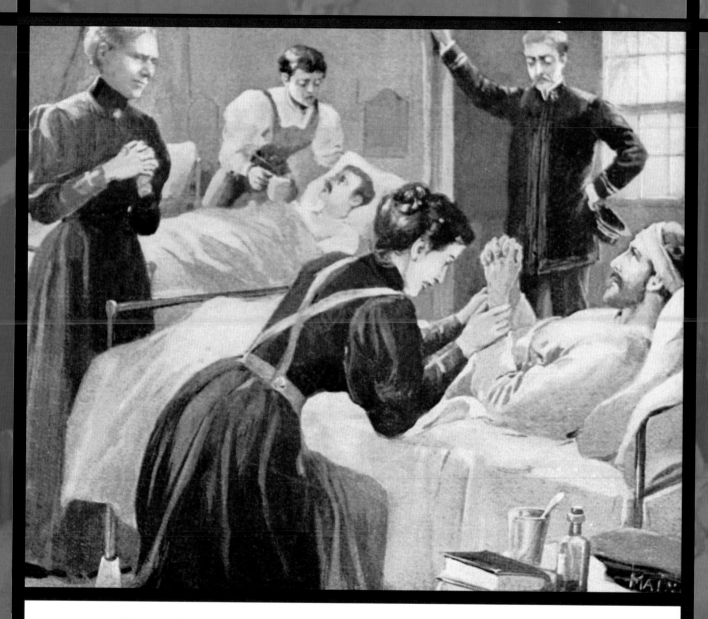

Many soldiers who survived the war told stories about Clara's kindness and her excellent nursing abilities, helping her legend grow throughout the country.

Even in old age, Clara kept working to help others. She founded the American Red Cross when she was sixty years old, and served as its president into her eighties.

At War's End

After the Civil War ended on April 9, 1865, Clara Barton chose another battle. It was the battle for human rights. She became a friend of Frederick Douglass, a black leader and former slave. Clara worked with him to gain rights for former slaves. Another friend of Clara's was Susan B. Anthony, a **suffragette**. Clara and Susan were determined to help women get the right to vote. While visiting Switzerland in 1869, Clara volunteered to help with an organization called the International Red Cross. This was a group that helped victims of war and other disasters around the world. She was so **impressed** with its work that she asked the founder if she could start a Red Cross Association in the United States.

The Red Cross

The rules that created the International Red Cross were a part of the 1864 **Treaty** of Geneva. Geneva is a city in Switzerland. Clara worked to convince lawmakers in the United States to accept the treaty so that she could found an American Red Cross. With President James Garfield's support, the United States signed the treaty. On May 21, 1881, Clara gathered a group of important people to help establish the first American Red Cross Society. Clara Barton served as the president of the American Red Cross for 22 years. The organization she helped to found continues today. On April 12, 1912, Clara died at the age of 90 and was buried in North Oxford, Massachusetts.

Glossary

addresses (A-drehs-ehz) Formal speeches.

career (kuh-REER) The work a person chooses to do.

Civil War (SIH-vul WOR) The war between the northern and southern states of the United States that was fought from 1861 to 1865.

Confederate (kun-FEH-deh-ret) The army for the South in the Civil War.

fevers (FEE-vuhrz) High body temperatures that occur when people are ill.

frivolous (FRIH-vul-us) Something that lacks seriousness or that is silly.

gruel (GROO-el) A thin mix of different foods.

humanitarian (hyoo-mah-nuh-TEHR-ee-uhn) Someone who works to help others.

impressed (im-PREST) To have had a strong effect on someone's feelings.

legend (LEH-jend) A story passed down through the years.

legendary (LEH-jen-der-ee) Famous and important.

legislature (LEH-juhs-lay-chur) A group of elected people who have the power to make the laws of a state or country.

obstacles (OB-stih-kulz) Things that are in the way.

rafters (RAF-terz) Beams below the ceiling that support the roof.

slavery (SLAY-vuh-ree) The system of one person owning another.

strategies (STRAH-tuh-jeez) The plans for war; plans for achieving a goal.

suffragette (suh-frih-JET) A woman who works for the right of women to vote.

survive (sur-VYV) To live longer than; to stay alive.

treaty (TREE-tee) A formal agreement between nations.

Union (YOON-yun) The northern states during the Civil War.

volunteers (vah-luhn-TEERZ) Workers who do not get paid for their work.

Index

Web Sites

To learn more about Clara Barton, check out these Web sites:
www.geocities.com/Athens/Aegean/6732/cb.html
www.redcross.org/hec/pre1900/cbarton.html